The Sec of Sailboat Racing

Mark Chisnell & Neal McDonald

fernhurst
B O O K S

www.fernhurstbooks.co.uk

NEAL MCDONALD First Class Honours BSc. Naval Architecture UCL

Member of UK Youth Squad for 3 years – 420 helm

1986	International 505 UK National Champion – Crew
1988	Olympics – 6th FD crew
1988	International 14 UK National Champion – Helm
1989	International 14 USA Champion – Helm
1989	International 14 World Champion – Helm
1989-93	Australian 18 Skiff professional circuit – Crew
1991-97	Ultra 30 circuit with Lawrie Smith – mainsheet
1991	Admiral's Cup on *Port Pendennis* – tactician & o/s helm
1991-96	Grand Prix Match racing circuit with Chris Law
1992-94	USA 50' Circuit on *Heaven Can Wait* – mainsheet
1994-95	America's Cup on Sydney 95 – mainsheet/tactician
1995	Admiral's Cup on *Rats on Fire* - mainsheet & o/s helm
1995	Southern Cross on *Ragamuffin* – tactician & o/s helm
1995-96	UK 18 Skiff circuit with Lawrie Smith – mainsheet
1997-98	Whitbread on *Silk Cut* – helmsman/trimmer
1998	49er European Champion
1998	Watch captain on *Stealth* when it made the monohull record for Marseilles to Tunisia
1998	7th in 49er World Championships, Melbourne
1999	British Admiral's Cup Team – mainsheet & offshore helm on *Venture 99* – (Farr 50)
1999	Cowes Week – tactician on *RSA* – the South African Erricson 80 – won Cowes week regatta
1999	Watch leader on *Stealth 99* Trans-Atlantic record attempt

MARK CHISNELL First Class Honours Physics and Philosophy, Nottingham

National Youth Squad

1984	Captain of Nottingham University Sailing Team
1986	*White Crusader* America's Cup Challenge – computer systems
1987	12 Metre World Championships – navigator
1988	Involved in development of Deckman on-board computer system
	Maxi Boat World Championships – 3 legs aboard *Congere*
	12 Metre World Championships – *White Crusader* – navigator
1989	*Jamarella* – won Admiral's Cup – top scoring boat
1990	International 14 European Championships
	Tornado World Championships
1991	*Port Pendennis*. Third in One Ton Cup, second in class Admiral's Cup – navigator
1992	Olympic Trials in 470
1993	*Swing* in Admiral's Cup – navigator
	Ragamuffin in Southern Cross – navigator
	IACC World Championship. Second in *Nippon* – navigator
1995	*No Problem* (Mumm 36) 2nd Mumm 36 Worlds – navigator
1997	Sail Clinic column in Practical Boat Owner
	Race Commentator on official Whitbread website
	Madina Milano (Farr IMS 49) Won Fastnet race
1998	Offshore News column in Yachts & Yachting
	Brava – overall team prize Sardinia Cup – navigator
1999	*Merit Cup* (Sydney 40) first World Championship, first in class Admiral's Cup – navigator

© Mark Chisnell & Neal McDonald
First published 2000 by Fernhurst Books
Duke's Path, High Street, Arundel, West Sussex BN18 9AJ, UK.
Tel: 01903 882277
Fax: 01903 882715
Email: sales@fernhurstbooks.co.uk
Website: www.fernhurstbooks.co.uk

Contact the publisher for a free, full-colour brochure.

British Library cataloguing in Publication Data: A catalogue
record for this book is available from the British Library.

ISBN 1 898660 72 7

Printed and bound in China through World Print

Design by Creative Byte

Cover design by Simon Balley

**For the latest news on our titles, offers and prices
visit our website: www.fernhurstbooks.co.uk**

CONTENTS

Introduction

There is a saying - 'Sailing is a simple sport, made complex by idiots'. Like most sayings, it isn't the whole story, but it contains some truth. This book has distilled the sport of sailboat racing down to a list of simple do's and don'ts, grouped together and ordered. But like the saying, these simple truths aren't the whole answer. For one thing, there are as many ways to lose sailboat races as there are sailors. Nor is there an outline in this book for the complex software necessary to design an America's Cup winner. But doing one of the don'ts in these pages has caused more than one promising America's Cup campaign to go off the rails. Races and regattas tend to be lost, rather than won - as true of the Club Championship as the Olympic Gold. Avoiding the simple mistakes, like the ones listed here, will go a long way to creating winners in everything from Optimists to Maxi Yachts.

Teams and Crews

Honest, clear communication is essential to every
successful programme - both ashore and on board.
It is important to create a structure for both, so that people
understand how the lines of communication work.

A winning team is more than the sum of its parts.

On the boat, everyone should know who ought
to be talking to whom, and about what.

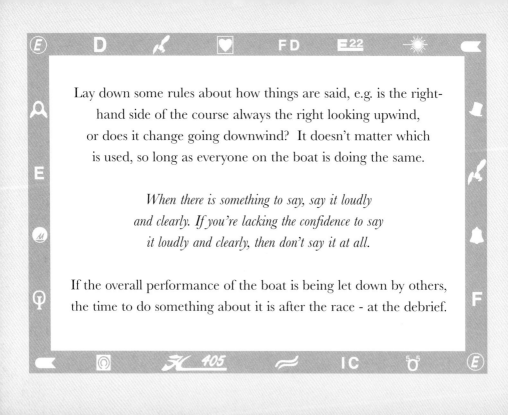

Lay down some rules about how things are said, e.g. is the right-hand side of the course always the right looking upwind, or does it change going downwind? It doesn't matter which is used, so long as everyone on the boat is doing the same.

When there is something to say, say it loudly and clearly. If you're lacking the confidence to say it loudly and clearly, then don't say it at all.

If the overall performance of the boat is being let down by others, the time to do something about it is after the race - at the debrief.

Make sure every practice and race day is
structured with a prep talk and a debrief.
Then everyone knows what is happening before the
action starts, and the whole crew has an opportunity
to say their piece at the end of the day.
Do any assigned job as well as possible.

*Starting to do other peoples' jobs during
the race will upset them, as well as hindering
personal concentration.*

Don't talk badly about fellow crew members behind their backs.

Money may be the root of all evil,
according to the proverb, but it's also the root of a great
deal of success and failure in sailboat racing.

The golden rules are:
1. Pick a goal that matches the finance available.
2. Always be clear in all dealings with crew,
skippers and owners. Make sure everyone
knows who is paying for what before the
season starts. Confusion can lead to
bad feeling, which can easily derail the sailing.

If the boat is going out training, then make sure there is a plan. People are much more willing to practise when they can see that the time is being used constructively.

At the same time it's important to vary the training to keep everyone interested. Fifteen gybes may be great fun for the helmsman, trimmers and foredeck, but the people on the runners will be bored after three or four.

Similarly, sailing upwind for hours on end will not keep the foredeck motivated. It is also better to have several short sessions than one long one - people work harder.

Don't be late for appointments,
especially arriving at the boat.
Nine people waiting for ten minutes is an
hour and a half of boat working time wasted.

Don't start racing a dinghy with an overall crew weight
different from the top performers in the class.
It's too easy to start relying on the weather
to excuse bad performance and, before long,
there will be no point bothering in anything
other than the 'optimum' conditions.

If there is a problem with the boat or crew,
talk about it to everyone involved. It's always better
to get it out into the open at the appropriate time.

If the boat has a big crew, they are all important.
It is the skipper's job to make sure that everyone feels valued.

Shouting at someone else on the boat
– beyond the moment for immediate,
urgent remedial action – is to be avoided.
It's never productive.

When sailing on a big boat,
don't start lunch between races (on a multi-race day)
until the boat is completely ready for the next race.
If one or two people are still packing spinnakers while
everyone else is eating lunch, team spirit suffers.

In a yacht going offshore,
make sure everyone knows there are limits
to the kit they can bring aboard.
With modern clothing technology, all that's required is
a set of thin thermals, mid-layer and foul weather gear.

At the end of the day, everyone should help pack up the boat.
On a yacht the tactician, helmsman or navigator
can help fold up a couple of sails. It makes a lot of
difference to the people who have been doing it all day.
It's the same for dinghy helms. Don't wander off
as soon as the boat is at the top of the ramp,
and let the crew pack it up.
If it is a yacht, then try and do it all before the boat
is back in the marina. Having the sails packed and the
running rigging cleared away before the boat is tied up
makes the crew look slick and professional.
And then everyone can go straight home - or to the beer tent!

On a multi-race day at least one person
must concentrate between races.
It's easy to get too far from the committee boat,
to miss the guns, or even run aground or capsize
and not be ready for the next start.

It is only possible to sail the race from where the boat is now.
It is not possible to sail the race from
where it would be, if it wasn't for that
windshift / breakage / bad mark rounding ten minutes ago.
So don't cry over spilt milk.

Body and Mind

Body and mind are important; the boat will struggle to sail without them.

Always drink plenty of water - even when it's cold and wet. Plain water is much better than anything else, but a little bit of fruit juice mixed in can make it a lot easier to drink. Dehydration degrades the body's physical and mental performance long before you start to feel thirsty. We are what we eat (and drink), so think about diet. Try and eat as early as possible before a race, and as soon as it's finished. The quicker the body gets food to replace energy that has been burned, the better the recovery it makes for the next day.

Always put on suitable footwear.

*In high-performance boats it's just as important to warm-up
and down, and stretch, as it is for a game of squash or football.*

Fitness is an important part of sailing, but it's not the whole game.
Try to keep the amount of time spent on physical training relative
to the job on the boat. For a grinder on an America's Cup boat,
physical fitness is everything. For most dinghy sailors,
a moderate level of fitness definitely helps.
Don't be fooled by those who appear to do nothing
except smoke and drink - they're fitter than they look.

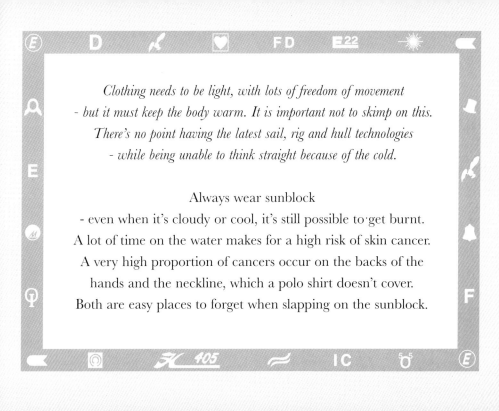

*Clothing needs to be light, with lots of freedom of movement
- but it must keep the body warm. It is important not to skimp on this.
There's no point having the latest sail, rig and hull technologies
- while being unable to think straight because of the cold.*

Always wear sunblock
- even when it's cloudy or cool, it's still possible to get burnt.
A lot of time on the water makes for a high risk of skin cancer.
A very high proportion of cancers occur on the backs of the
hands and the neckline, which a polo shirt doesn't cover.
Both are easy places to forget when slapping on the sunblock.

Always wear sunglasses or shade the eyes with a peaked hat.
Eyes are just as vulnerable to sun damage as skin, and they are even
more important. It's worth spending money on good quality sunglasses.
Try a few pairs first - getting something comfortable,
with the right lenses, makes them more likely to be worn.
If you're worried about losing glasses or hats, use string or buy one
of the smart proprietary attachments (i.e. croakies).

The bigger the boat, the more important it is to keep body
parts away from sheaves, blocks and loaded ropes.
Limbs and fingers can get sucked in frighteningly easily
if someone eases or tightens something unexpectedly.

Be careful with cuts and scrapes.
If they are constantly getting wet, leaving them unattended
can turn a simple graze into something that could lose a regatta.
It's also important to keep up-to-date with tetanus jabs and,
when travelling, checking for all the right inoculations.

When offshore, always take off foul weather gear
when down below and off-watch
- even if it is just for half an hour.
It gives the body and the bunks more chance
to dry out and stay dry.

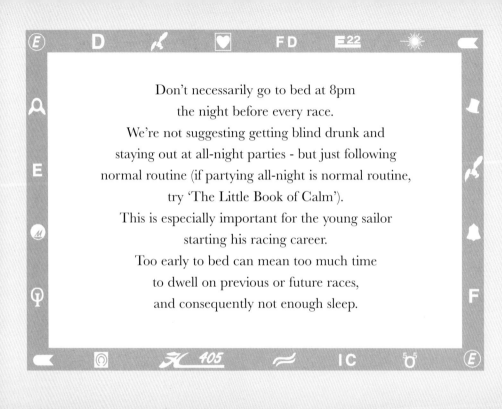

Don't necessarily go to bed at 8pm
the night before every race.
We're not suggesting getting blind drunk and
staying out at all-night parties - but just following
normal routine (if partying all-night is normal routine,
try 'The Little Book of Calm').
This is especially important for the young sailor
starting his racing career.
Too early to bed can mean too much time
to dwell on previous or future races,
and consequently not enough sleep.

Boat Preparation

*Stick with the KIS principle
- Keep It Simple.*

Establish a routine for rigging the boat,
and for checking that everything is led correctly.
Doing things in the same order
will make it easier to learn - write it down
if that makes it easier to establish the routine.

Don't take risks with any fittings or equipment that are directly responsible for holding the mast up, and the keel and rudder on.

Calibrate sail settings as much as possible - sheet positions, outhaul and so on. If possible, use numbers that have a real meaning - angle of rudder to the centreline, or the angle of the headsail (jib, for dinghy sailors) lead to the centreline. With a non-overlapping headsail, marking the underside of the spreaders means the leech position can be repeated easily.

Do take a look at other people's gear failures and breakages.
Similar equipment may fail the same way.

Reducing the weight of the boat is important, particularly
weight from the bow and stern, and from the rig.
If there is a minimum class weight for the boat,
she must be down to that weight.
But this must be achieved without compromising reliability.

On a dinghy, the mast should be straight sideways
when it is set up with full rig tension on the trolley.
The best view is to look up the mainsail track.
Pulling a thin line tight from masthead
to heel plug will provide a comparison.
It will never be straight side-to-side when the boat is sailing.

The rudder is a common point of gear failure in dinghies. The loading on the lower fitting is greater than that on the top, and consequently the bottom fitting is the most likely failure point. In foam sandwich rudders, the foam can be crushed if the fitting is over-tightened. The solution is to drill the fastening holes out to a larger size, fill them with a mix of epoxy and filler powder, then re-drill the holes for the bolts.

Check that the mast is upright in the boat when not sailing. The simplest way is to measure from the top of the mast to a fixed point or points on either side of the boat. Be careful that the tape is stretched the same amount for each measurement.

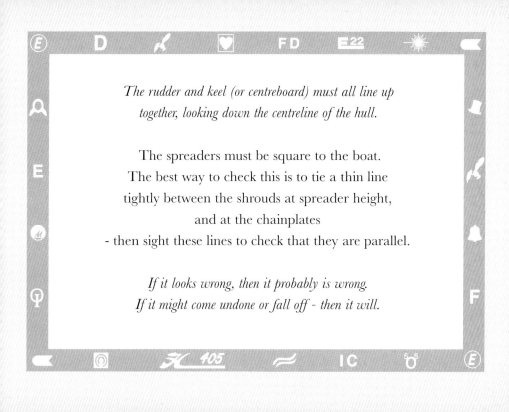

*The rudder and keel (or centreboard) must all line up
together, looking down the centreline of the hull.*

The spreaders must be square to the boat.
The best way to check this is to tie a thin line
tightly between the shrouds at spreader height,
and at the chainplates
- then sight these lines to check that they are parallel.

*If it looks wrong, then it probably is wrong.
If it might come undone or fall off - then it will.*

On a yacht, with fractional or masthead rig, the goal of rig tuning is to keep the mast straight sideways when sailing upwind.

Hull and foil finish are important - not just the surface finish, but also the fairness. The foils are the most important, then the front of the hull, and then the back. The argument is still raging over the advantages of matt and polished finishes. But never finish a surface with wet and dry rougher than 400 grade.

The headsail leads must be the same distance from the tack fitting.

Always carry a knife. On a dinghy it might be taped to the boom. On a yacht carry it on a belt or in a pocket. The modern multi-tools (Leatherman, Gerber) do an excellent job as both knife and emergency tool-kit.

Make absolutely sure that sail battens are not going to fly out when the sail flogs. That might mean stitching them in.

Always have a minimum tool-kit with the boat. For a dinghy this might be a shackle key, some rope and a knife. On a yacht it's screwdrivers, adjustable spanners and a hacksaw (with plenty of spare blades).

Always pay particular attention to gear that could rip a spinnaker, and tape or cover it. Spreader ends, fittings around the vang and the ends of battens in the headsail are all good candidates.

There are often better ways of fastening fittings
than using shackles, which are expensive,
heavy and can come undone.
A strop made from webbing material,
properly hand stitched, is lighter and allows
more movement to the fitting that is attached to it.

In a yacht with a speedo try to get hold of a set of performance tables from the designer or builder - usually called polars. Update them after every sail. They are especially useful when racing offshore or at night.

When it is in contact with carbon fibre, aluminium is even more likely to corrode than when it is in contact with stainless steel. In both cases, the materials must be separated with a suitable barrier - such as plastic or a layer of glassfibre. A good example is the aluminium end fitting on a carbon spinnaker pole.

It is possible to put too many purchases in a control system like the vang or cunningham. The extra mechanical advantage from the blocks can be outweighed by the extra friction.

Sometimes a control system like the vang can be made to run more smoothly by reducing the diameter of the rope, or by increasing the diameter of the sheaves.

Rope isn't just rope any more. Modern high-tech fibres (new ones are developed all the time) have very specific properties. It's important to choose the right rope for each job.

*If the boat has electrical systems, make sure
the batteries are well-charged before the race starts.
Turning the engine on to charge them is noisy and distracting.*

On a yacht, make sure that there are two separate battery banks,
one for the boat's equipment, the other to start the engine or
generator. Then, even if the supply batteries are run flat,
it will be possible to start the engine and recharge.
If the battery switch can link both banks of batteries
together for normal use - don't let it!

When working aloft, check that all the tools used are attached to the body, or the harness. One easy thing to forget is the battery in a cordless drill - tape it in.

Check the load-carrying capacity of all fittings or hardware in any given system on the boat (cunningham, vang, etc) to see if there are any weak links. There is no point having all the blocks capable of taking five hundred kilos of load, if the cleat will fail at two hundred kilos.

The weakest link in the system should be the easiest thing to replace or repair - usually the rope.

Don't trust the instrument system unless,
or until, it has been calibrated properly.
This applies as much to the twin compasses on
a dinghy's sidedecks as it does to a full-blown yacht system.

Tie a knot in the end of halyards, sheets and control lines.
(Never tie the knot at the end of the rope
- always leave something to grab hold of,
when it's run out to the end.)
But, on yachts, don't tie a knot in the
ends of spinnaker sheets or guys.

On a yacht racing in tidal waters,
if there is a chance of light air make sure the boat
is set up for 'tactical anchoring' with a good kedging anchor.
The anchor line should be three times longer
than the deepest water on the racecourse.
Because it's only used in light air and probably flat water,
it needn't be that strong - eight millimetre polypropylene is
enough even for fifty foot yachts, and it doesn't absorb water.
Don't forget some chain, to get it to hold,
and a shorter conventional anchor warp
for rough weather and shallow water.

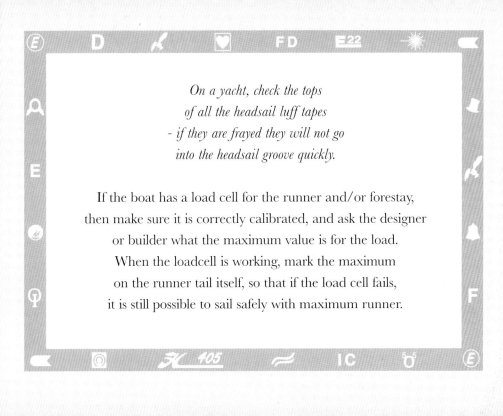

On a yacht, check the tops
of all the headsail luff tapes
- if they are frayed they will not go
into the headsail groove quickly.

If the boat has a load cell for the runner and/or forestay,
then make sure it is correctly calibrated, and ask the designer
or builder what the maximum value is for the load.
When the loadcell is working, mark the maximum
on the runner tail itself, so that if the load cell fails,
it is still possible to sail safely with maximum runner.

Boatspeed and Sail Trim

Boatspeed makes a tactical genius.

It rarely pays to re-invent the wheel
- using the same gear as the fast guys in the fleet
means that, at the very least, the boat won't be slow.
When new to a class, talk to the top two or three
sailmakers and read their tuning guides
- they are often full of useful pointers.

Look at new sails before racing with them,
to check that the sailmaker has delivered what was ordered,
and to test their speed.

Don't use new gear for the first time in a big regatta.

It's unrealistic to strive to be the fastest boat in the fleet in
all conditions. Such a search can lead to radical options
that end up being slow, or only fast in one set of conditions.
Aim to have boatspeed within the top ten percent of the fleet
in all conditions, and the ability to switch smoothly between
set-ups for different conditions.

Always take an opportunity to look at the sails and
rig from off the boat. They often appear quite different
- both to what's expected, and to the competition.

Time management is a boring old buzz word.
But the quicker that lessons can be absorbed from each boat, sail, race and
venue - the quicker improvements will be made. There is no substitute for
keeping notes, in a system which will allow for the retrieval of the right
information at the right time. A computer is the best place to do it, perhaps
on a spreadsheet or a database. Failing that a solid hardback book will do.
On a keelboat have a wetnote book to keep notes, and make a job list.
On a dinghy, use a chinagraph on some tape on the deck.

The real trick to sailing fast is sailing in the right mode
at the right time - high and slow or low and fast.
The difference is subtle, maybe only a couple of degrees
in wind angle. Two boat tuning and careful observation
are the only ways to be confident of the differences.
Wind and sea conditions, and the boats nearby,
will dictate the mode.

*Just as important as sailing in the right mode is
having everyone on the boat sailing in the same mode.
Good communication between the sail trimmers and helm is crucial.*

*Never underestimate how important it is to sail the boat
at the optimum angle of heel. Particularly in a dinghy,
doing this all the time is incredibly difficult and probably
the biggest single difference between those who seem effortlessly
quick in any boat they get into, and the rest of us.*

Achieving the optimum angle of heel in a dinghy is not just
about steering and trimming, it is also about rig set-up.
The rig must work for the crew, not against them.
Look around the fleet to see who is sailing their boat
the most upright, with the least effort on the mainsheet
- they have the rig set up properly.

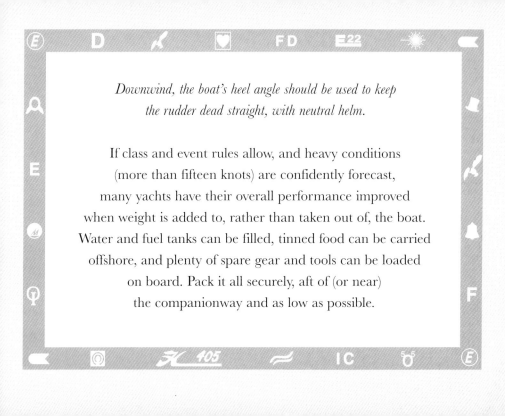

Downwind, the boat's heel angle should be used to keep the rudder dead straight, with neutral helm.

If class and event rules allow, and heavy conditions (more than fifteen knots) are confidently forecast, many yachts have their overall performance improved when weight is added to, rather than taken out of, the boat. Water and fuel tanks can be filled, tinned food can be carried offshore, and plenty of spare gear and tools can be loaded on board. Pack it all securely, aft of (or near) the companionway and as low as possible.

Just because the spinnaker is full at a tight reaching angle
in light air doesn't necessarily mean that it is the fastest sail.
The rule of thumb is: it's quicker with the headsail at any
apparent wind angle under 65 degrees.

*Weed on the foils will slow the boat dramatically. Always reverse the
boat before the start, or pull up the rudder and centreboard in a dinghy.
Keep a good look-out ahead of the boat, and keep checking the foils.*

When practising, try to avoid using really old sails.
Using equipment that is like the racing gear means
you'll rapidly get used to setting it up and adjusting it.

Always check that the leeward twinning line
is completely eased when you're reaching
with the spinnaker up.

On a yacht, always carry a weed-stick
- a long batten with about half a metre
of sail tie or thick rope attached to the end.
Stab it down in front of the rudder at the top,
and push the sail tie down the leading edge.

On a yacht, always carry a weed rope
- about twenty or thirty feet of rope with a knot at
three foot intervals. Coil the rope, and with the tail in
one hand, throw the coils round the bow to leeward.
The boat sails over it; hold onto the tail and run
down the weather side, pulling and easing the rope.
The other end will be round the other side of the keel,
and as it works across the leading edge,
the knots will dislodge the weed.

When the wind is going up and down,
set up the rig for the lulls, not the gusts.

Boat Handling

Keep the mast pointing at the sky!

It's almost always smarter to drop a spinnaker early,
rather than late. The potential losses of a bad rounding
- spinnaker half up and headsail flapping
- are much greater than the loss of not having
the spinnaker pulling for the final boat-length.

If the boat is unstable running downwind in a breeze and waves,
sheet the mainsail on, let the spinnaker pole forward and sail
a touch higher to make it easier to control.

Never let the sails flog more than necessary.
Apart from wearing them out the noise is distracting,
and in a big breeze it can be unsettling for inexperienced crew.
If the sails are flapping, be very wary of them.
Even small sails can be dangerous in a strong breeze.
If the sails must flap, keep tension on the sheets
to stop the sheets wrapping around each other.

Boat Handling - Dinghies

Always have the jibsheet out of the cleat
before the helmsman starts to tack.

*Always ease the vang before trying to bear
away at the weather mark.*

Small boat-handling errors can often escalate into major ones
- like a capsize. If something unsettling happens,
a knot in a sheet perhaps, focus on the priorities first
- keeping the boat upright.

Try to steer the boat with as little rudder as possible
- which means using the heel angle to help the rudder.
Sailing without a rudder in light airs is excellent practice.

*A lot of grief can be saved by a glance at the mainsheet tail before the
windward mark, and at the spinnaker halyard tail before the leeward mark.*

In moderate and strong breeze,
confidence and decisiveness must start as soon as the boat
is launched. This confidence only really comes with practice.
In dinghies, better boat handling, through time on the water,
is a swift way to move off the back of the fleet.

It's quicker not to capsize at all

– but everybody does, particularly in modern high
performance boats. So practice recovering from a capsize,
in the actual conditions in which it's most likely to happen.

Develop strategies for the fastest way
to get the boat back upright.

The potential range of differences in helm and
crew weight mean that these are specific to each crew.

Work out a plan for all the major potential situations
– capsizing to windward/leeward, with the spinnaker up/down,
helmsman/crew falls in to windward/leeward – and so on.

*When gybing in a strong breeze remember
that the faster the boat is going, the safer it is.
The best time is to gybe while surfing flat out on a wave,
with the sails unloaded.*

If the rig is fully depowered and you're still
overpowered pull up the centreboard or daggerboard.
Most dinghies will sail faster upwind in these conditions
with as little as half of the board in the water,
and be more controllable.

Boat Handling - Yachts

In a broach, never let off the guy. If you do, the spinnaker
will blow to leeward and hold the boat on its side.

Hoisting a spinnaker that is twisted is slow.
Whoever packs the sail (it should always be the same person)
must take the time to do it properly
- however much they are needed back on the rail.
Try to pack the sail in a lull, or flat water, not during
a desperate struggle to make a leebow tack work.

In a yacht with both backstay and runners, always remember to let the backstay off before the runners are eased when bearing away.

Never take the slack out of the vang
when going upwind in a keelboat.
Forgetting that the vang is tight at the windward mark,
or when easing the main to duck another boat upwind, could
break the boom - not to mention a major loss of control.

*It may be necessary in medium and strong winds to
ease the headsail to get a yacht flat enough to bear away.
Otherwise the heel angle over-rides the balance of the sail trim.*

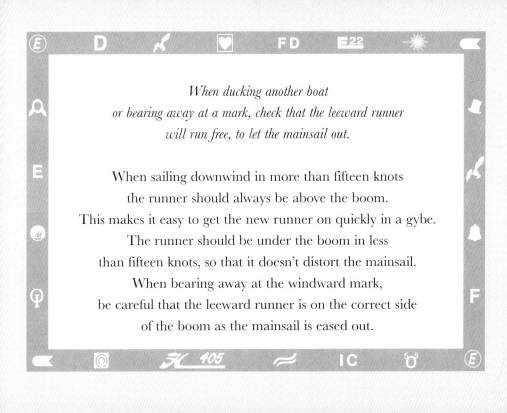

When ducking another boat
or bearing away at a mark, check that the leeward runner
will run free, to let the mainsail out.

When sailing downwind in more than fifteen knots
the runner should always be above the boom.
This makes it easy to get the new runner on quickly in a gybe.
The runner should be under the boom in less
than fifteen knots, so that it doesn't distort the mainsail.
When bearing away at the windward mark,
be careful that the leeward runner is on the correct side
of the boom as the mainsail is eased out.

Sending a person up the mast, particularly at sea, is a dangerous business. But because it happens so often it is easy to get complacent about it. Make sure that everyone involved, tailing and bouncing halyards as well as fastening harnesses and halyards, knows what they are doing. Never trust a shackle of any kind. A double bowline or climbing knot is the only safe way of securing a harness or boson's chair to a halyard. Trimmers and drivers should take extra care in any sort of breeze - a wipe-out with someone up the mast is very dangerous.

When racing offshore and sailing on the same leg for some time, put a second, safety sheet onto headsails and spinnakers.

When sailing downwind with the leeward runner pulled forward under the boom, always check that the runner is not fouled on the spreaders before gybing or tacking - especially at night.

Don't stand to leeward and aft of a spinnaker that is being dropped. It could take you overboard with it if it doesn't come down smoothly, goes in the water, or blows free.

Always beware of the lazy spinnaker sheet, don't stand over it or put a foot or hand in a loop. If the guy breaks or slips, the lazy sheet will suddenly go tight.

When racing offshore at night,
take a peek over the side every hour or so to make sure
nothing is trailing in the water and slowing the boat down.
It is also possible to lose crucial gear over the side.

When moving around a yacht downwind,
always be conscious that winches may suddenly
need to be wound. Disturbing the sheet between
the trimmer and the winch,
or getting in the way of the grinder,
can end up with the spinnaker flogging.

*On a yacht with runners ensure that one of them is pulled
all the way forward to the shrouds, before hoisting the mainsail.
Steer the boat just off head-to-wind, to keep the
flogging mainsail on the side with no runner.*

If there is a gear problem and only a couple of people
are required to fix it, it is crucial that everyone else lets them
get on with it and concentrates on racing the boat.
Not only is advice usually unhelpful, but if the boat makes
a tactical error because no one is watching the racecourse
a small initial problem can be massively compounded.

Offshore Survival Sailing

The radio may well be a lifeline.
More than one person must know how to use it properly.

If the crew look after the boat, the boat will look after the crew.

Always carry a personal strobe light on offshore races.
Keep it in your foul weather jacket pocket.

Whenever racing offshore on a new boat,
or with a new crew,
personally check all the safety equipment before leaving.
It won't help to blame someone else if it cuts up rough
and the harnesses are frayed and the flares out-of-date.

When packing the trysail it is worth rolling it in a vertical sausage.
Leave the luff slides or bolt rope accessible,
and secure the sail thoroughly with wool.
Then it can be brought on deck and hoisted
under control, without flapping.
The wools are broken when everything is ready.

Always practise putting up storm sails, before they are needed for real.

Always step *up* into the liferaft.

*Make sure that the storm sails are strong enough,
and in good enough condition to survive anything.
Cheap or worn out sails can be life threatening,
failing at exactly the moment they are most needed.*

All the crew must know where the various pieces of safety
equipment are stored, how to use them, how to mark a man
overboard position on the GPS, and how to start the engine.

*Many people have fallen off boats when trying to use
the transom as a lavatory in heavy weather.
It's difficult to hold on, and the motion is more severe at the stern than
anywhere else on the boat (except on the bow). Use the cockpit or,
if it's really rough, have a bottle tied to the companionway ladder that
can be used inside the boat, and then emptied into the cockpit.*

If the main is left on the boom when the trysail is set, roll it
and tie it down as tightly as possible. If the yacht has a solid vang,
then put a halyard on the end of the boom to act as a topping
lift and hold the boom up. One good wave landing in the rolled
mainsail can compress a solid vang until it crumples.

When it gets really wild, above forty knots
and in big seas, it's not worth having people on the rail.
Waves can snap off stanchions,
and people can fall a long way into the boat.
Leave four or five crew on deck to sail the boat,
and get everyone else below to try and rest.
Keep some crew on standby, ready to go on deck.
Make sure a proper watch system is operating.
And modify it carefully if any of the crew
are debilitated by seasickness.

Those prone to seasickness must look after themselves.
No greasy foods before or during the race.
Sleep well beforehand. Try the proprietary sea-sickness tablets
to find one that works, and take them in plenty of time.
Drink to replace the fluids lost. It's always better on deck,
with a view of the horizon. That's also why dark nights
and fog are unpleasant. Doing something on deck helps.
Avoid standing or sitting up below decks. When going below
to rest, get horizontal in a bunk quickly. When putting on foul
weather gear below, try and lie on a bunk to do it.
Get someone who isn't prone to the problem
to do any work that must be done below.

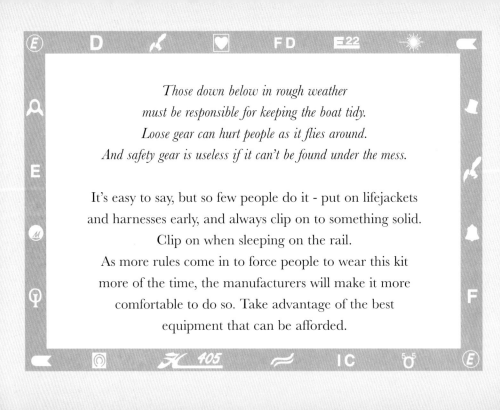

Those down below in rough weather
must be responsible for keeping the boat tidy.
Loose gear can hurt people as it flies around.
And safety gear is useless if it can't be found under the mess.

It's easy to say, but so few people do it - put on lifejackets
and harnesses early, and always clip on to something solid.
Clip on when sleeping on the rail.
As more rules come in to force people to wear this kit
more of the time, the manufacturers will make it more
comfortable to do so. Take advantage of the best
equipment that can be afforded.

If there is strong wind forecast for a long offshore race,
take a spare main if the rules allow it.
The weight won't hurt in the bilge.

When white sail reaching in heavy air, it's a good idea to put
the flattening reef in (if the boat has one). Keeping the boom
out of the water may save it from breaking.

Take the leeward runner all the way forward to the mast before
putting in or shaking out a reef - otherwise the flogging mainsail
will try its best to tangle up the reef lines with the runner.

Dinghy Survival Sailing

*Recognise that the wind is now so strong that staying upright
is enough to get a good finishing position – and adapt.*

Minimise and simplify all manoeuvres
– go with just one tack and one gybe per leg,
and make sure they are done on a safe layline.

Don't rush anything;
anticipate tactical boat-on-boat
situations and as far as possible avoid them.
Being forced to manoeuvre to dodge
another boat means a seriously increased risk of capsize.

If physically possible, don't cleat any sheets.
Having the ability to ease them instantly
is more important than having them trimmed perfectly.

Always assume any boats nearby are about to spin
out of control, and onto a collision course.

When choosing the side of the course to sail, remember to try and avoid rough water (tide or shallows may make it worse in one particular area).

Make the decision to tack round – rather than gybe – early.
The manoeuvre requires just as much
anticipation and commitment as gybing.
It's essential to do it quickly, to sheet on,
trim and hike through the luff and to
have enough speed to get through the wind.
Sail far enough past the mark before tacking
to avoid a big bear away after the tack.

Tactics and Strategy

Know the course.

Research the regatta venue thoroughly.
If you're a dinghy sailor don't ignore the useful information
in cruising and pilot books, and on Admiralty charts.

*Always find or arrange a source for
a proper local weather forecast.*

It is essential to understand
the workings of current and tide
– especially the way they modify the sailing wind
– and how to use them to create advantage.

Always read the sailing instructions
and notice of race.

If nobody on the boat knows the flags
buy a sticker with them on
and display it in the cockpit.

Anticipation is the key to smooth sailing.
Things are much more likely to go wrong
when a situation comes as a surprise.
Keep thinking through possible scenarios.

Don't get too far from the start-line area,
especially if the boat hasn't got an engine.

There are three fundamental components to a good start.
All three are almost always more important
than being right at the favoured end of the line,
or precisely on the line at the gun.

1. Clear air.
2. Speed.
3. Freedom to choose a strategy and a sailing mode,
rather than have them dictated by others.

If the regatta is using gate starts, there are several factors in deciding whether to go late or early:
1. If there is a clear choice as to which side of the course is advantaged.
   E.g. if the right-hand side has a wind or current advantage – start late.
2. If you have a big speed differential to the gate boat in today's conditions.
   If the gate boat is slow – start early.
   If the gate boat is quick – start late.
3. If it is shifty, consider starting early to take advantage of the oscillations.

When starting at a gate start, the rules are simple:

1. Start at maximum speed and on the wind, right on the guard boat. The worst mistake is not being on the wind (apart from hitting the guard or gate boat!).

2. Start with someone slower to leeward, with as big a gap as possible.

Develop a strategy early for the theoretically favoured side of each beat and run, and modify it with observation as the race develops. With no other ideas for a strategy, position the boat for the inside berth at the next mark when going downwind. Going upwind, stay to the right of the nearest competition, to have the starboard tack approach to the mark.

Risk management.

Sounds trendy, but it's an important way of looking at the race.
Big chances are only worth taking when there are equally big
gains to be made. And the most likely times to make big gains are
off the start-line and on the first beat and run.
If a beat is up a shoreline against the tide,
then there is a huge reward for getting in
as close as possible on the first few tacks,
compared to the losses of running aground.
But by the final beat, with only a boat or two close by,
there are few gains to be made from pushing it.

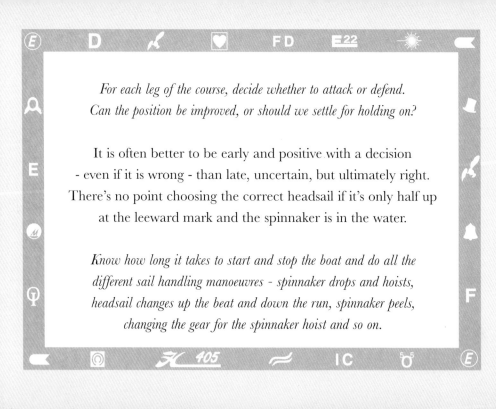

For each leg of the course, decide whether to attack or defend.
Can the position be improved, or should we settle for holding on?

It is often better to be early and positive with a decision
- even if it is wrong - than late, uncertain, but ultimately right.
There's no point choosing the correct headsail if it's only half up
at the leeward mark and the spinnaker is in the water.

Know how long it takes to start and stop the boat and do all the
different sail handling manoeuvres - spinnaker drops and hoists,
headsail changes up the beat and down the run, spinnaker peels,
changing the gear for the spinnaker hoist and so on.

Don't be late for the start.
And try and get to the start area the same time every day.
Many regattas start the first day with
the entire fleet out two hours early.
But by the end, barely half the fleet are there on time.
Establish a routine and stick to it,
no matter which day of the regatta it is.

If you're having a reasonable race
keep a position somewhere between
the majority of the fleet and the next mark.

Tacking upwind or gybing downwind,
the leg is sometimes set so that there is more
time on one tack than the other.
It is always safer to sail the longest tack or gybe first,
which will keep you closer to the mark.

On a triangle course,
always gybe at the gybe mark unless
you are confident of spending a significant
amount of time on the other gybe.

When there are twin leeward marks,
and either can be rounded,
the priorities in choosing which to go for are:
1. No other boats in front, i.e. clear air after the rounding;
2. Heading the right way without having to tack;
3. The buoy with the shortest distance to the windward mark.

*For a yacht that is not fully powered-up with
all the crew hiking, and a dinghy that is not planing,
then finding more wind is almost always more important
than being on the favoured tack for the windshift.*

*The wind doesn't stop shifting
when sailing downwind.
Shifts are just as important on the run, especially
in high performance boats that sail wide angles.*

Use transits as much as possible when the land
is close enough to provide them. Particularly:
• On the start line, to know where the line is;
• When trying to cross another boat;
• When approaching a mark in tide;
• When trying to judge if another boat is quicker or slower.

Stay away from the laylines to the mark
for as long as possible.
But also remember:
doing too many tacks is slow.
Find the appropriate compromise
for the boat and the conditions.

If you're tacking across a bay,
or along a shoreline, always tack in towards
a headland or point whenever possible.

Don't underestimate tactical anchoring in tidal waters.

Some rules:

1. When going backwards (the GPS or a transit will provide the confirmation) get the anchor out immediately.

2. If it is possible to go sideways towards an area of more wind, or more favourable tide, then do it, rather than anchor. It may even be better to go backwards a little as well, if you're convinced the better breeze or tide is there.

3. If the tide is taking the boat to a mark, but is too strong to sail back into once the mark is rounded, then consider anchoring uptide, before the mark.

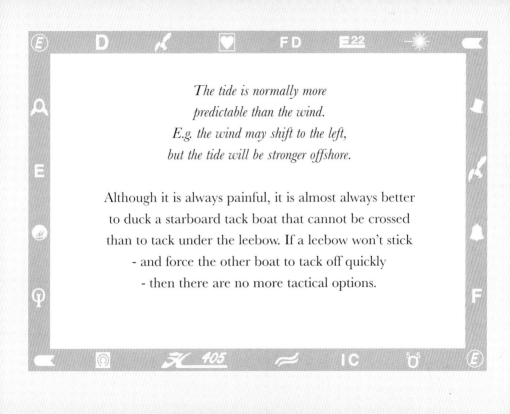

The tide is normally more
predictable than the wind.
E.g. the wind may shift to the left,
but the tide will be stronger offshore.

Although it is always painful, it is almost always better
to duck a starboard tack boat that cannot be crossed
than to tack under the leebow. If a leebow won't stick
- and force the other boat to tack off quickly
- then there are no more tactical options.

Try not to tack just after crossing
behind another boat or boats
- either tack before them or go several lengths
past their line before tacking.

Never tack under someone who is close to
the layline, but may not be on it.
Unless you're absolutely sure they are comfortably
laying the mark, duck behind them
and go on to a safe layline.

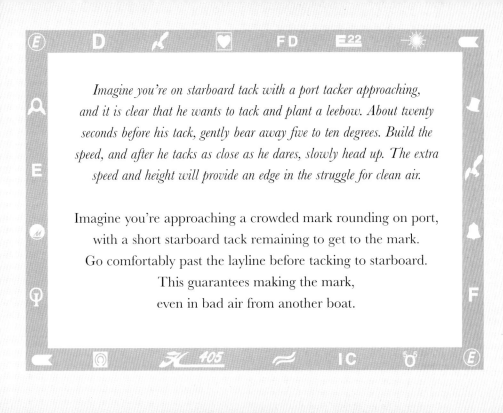

Imagine you're on starboard tack with a port tacker approaching, and it is clear that he wants to tack and plant a leebow. About twenty seconds before his tack, gently bear away five to ten degrees. Build the speed, and after he tacks as close as he dares, slowly head up. The extra speed and height will provide an edge in the struggle for clean air.

Imagine you're approaching a crowded mark rounding on port,
with a short starboard tack remaining to get to the mark.
Go comfortably past the layline before tacking to starboard.
This guarantees making the mark,
even in bad air from another boat.

Always defend clear air
early and vigorously on a reach,
particularly in big one-design fleets.
Long, slow luffs, that start
when the boat behind
is already to windward,
are counter-productive to both
defender and attacker.
Short sharp luffs mean business.

Protests and Rule Infringements

Keep out of the protest room.

Always take an interest in any protest decisions
made at regattas, and why they went the way they did.
Talk to those involved - it's a cheap way of getting
protest experience, without getting thrown out!

Always carry a proper protest flag.
On a yacht it should be attached to the pushpit,
top guardrail or backstay, and rolled up on it.
Don't furl it too securely - it may unfurl too slowly to satisfy
a protest committee. A single wrap of tape is best,
with a tag that can be grabbed quickly to pull it off.
If you're sailing a dinghy keep the flag in
a handy pocket where you can get at it in
a capsize resulting from a protestable incident.

Practice taking a 360° and a 720° penalty
- and always tell the crew what's happening.

If a situation is developing that may result in
a rules incident, make sure only one person
on the boat is communicating with the other boat.
Two people yelling conflicting instructions
(Starboard! You can cross!) is not good.

When in the wrong, take the penalty immediately
(after sailing clear). By the time most people have deliberated,
it is technically too late to accept the penalty
- and it is possible to end up taking a second one.

Even when you're a hundred percent
confident of winning a protest,
the chances are only
fifty/fifty once you're in The Room.

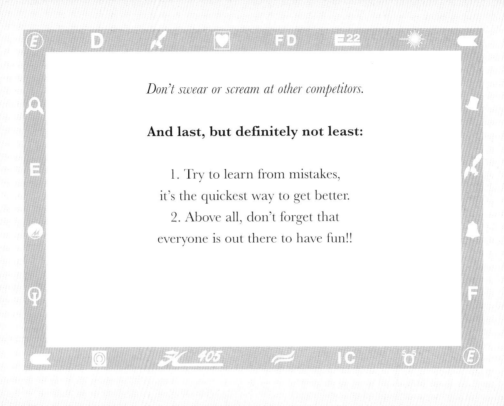

Don't swear or scream at other competitors.

And last, but definitely not least:

1. Try to learn from mistakes,
it's the quickest way to get better.
2. Above all, don't forget that
everyone is out there to have fun!!

"As sailors, we can always count on volunteer lifeboat crews. Can they count on you? Please join *Offshore* today."

Sir Robin Knox-Johnston CBE, RD*

However experienced you are at sea, you never know when you'll need the help of a lifeboat crew. But to keep saving lives, the Royal National Lifeboat Institution's volunteer crews need *your* help.

That is why you should join **Offshore**. For just £3.50 per month, you can help save thousands of lives, receive practical information to help keep *you* safe at sea *and* save money on equipment for your boat. *Please join us today.*

Please join *Offshore* – today

Please photocopy and return this form, with your payment if appropriate, to: RNLI, FREEPOST, West Quay Road, Poole, Dorset BH15 1XF.

Mr/Mrs/Miss/Ms [　　] Initial [　　] Surname [　　　　　　　　　　]

Address [　　　　　　　　　　]

[　　　　　　　　　　] Postcode [　　　]

I would like to join:

☐ **As an *Offshore* member at £** [　　] per month/quarter/year * (min £3.50 per month/£10 per quarter/£40 per year)

☐ **As Joint *Offshore* members at £** [　　] per month/quarter/year *

(Husband & Wife, min £6 per month/£17.50 per quarter/£70 per year) * please delete as applicable

Please debit the above sum as indicated from my Visa/MasterCard * now and at the prevailing rate until cancelled by me in writing.

Card No. [　　　　　　　　　　　　　　　　] Expiry date [　/　]

Signature [　　　　　　　　] (Please give address of cardholder on a separate piece of paper if different from above.)

Lifeboats
Offshore

Alternatively, I wish to pay my **Offshore** membership by cheque/PO

I enclose a cheque/Postal Order for **£** [　　] payable to Royal National Lifeboat Institution.

Or, I wish to pay my subscription by Direct Debit ☐

Please tick the box – a Direct Debit form will be sent to you.　　FERN8　　Registered Charity No. 209603

Because life's not all plain sailing

For a free, full-colour brochure write, phone or fax us at:

Fernhurst Books
Duke's Path, High Street, Arundel,
West Sussex BN18 9AJ, UK.

Tel: 01903 882277
Fax: 01903 882715
Email: sales@fernhurstbooks.co.uk
Website: www.fernhurstbooks.co.uk